Can you?

drive

cook

dance

swim

speak English

speak Spanish

play guitar

play soccer

What is she doing?

She is driving.

What is she doing?

She is cooking.

What are they doing?

They are dancing.

What are they doing?

They are swimming.

What is he doing?

He is speaking English.

What is he doing?

He is speaking Spanish.

What is he doing?

He is playing the guitar.

What are they doing?

They are playing soccer.

Can you drive?

No, I can't.

Can you cook?

Yes, I can.

Can you dance?

Yes, I can.

Can you swim?

No, I can't.

Can you speak English?

Yes, I can.

Can you speak Spanish?

No, I can't.

Can you play the guitar?

No, I can't.

Can you play soccer?

Yes, I can.

Easy English Readers:
Can you?

www.teachabcenglish.com

2016

Made in the USA
Middletown, DE
23 March 2018